What Does "Academic" Mean?

Josef Pieper Works from St. Augustine's Press

The Christian Idea of Man
Preface by John Haldane; trans. Dan Farrelly

The Concept of Sin
Trans. Edward A. Oaks, S.J.

Death and Immortality
Trans. Richard and Clara Winston

Enthusiasm and Divine Madness: On the Platonic Dialogue Phaedrus
Trans. Richard and Clara Winston

Happiness and Contemplation
Introduction by Ralph McInerny; trans. Richard and Clara Winston

In Tune with the World: A Theory of Festivity
Trans. Richard and Clara Winston

Not Yet the Twilight (vol. II of Pieper's autobiography)
Trans. Dan and Una Farrelly

The Platonic Myths
Introduction by James V. Schall; trans. Dan Farrelly

Scholasticism: Problems and Personalities of Medieval Philosophy
Trans. Richard and Clara Winston

The Silence of Goethe
Preface by Ralph McInerny; trans. Dan Farrelly

The Silence of St. Thomas: Three Essays
Trans. John Murray, S.J., and Danial O'Connor

Tradition: Concept and Claim
Trans. E. Christian Kopff

Tradition as Challenge: Essays and Speeches
Trans. Dan Farrelly

What Catholics Believe (with Heinz Raskop)
Introduction by Gerald B. Phelan; trans. Christopher Huntington

The Story – Where Will It End? (vol. III of Pieper's autobiography)
Trans. Dan and Una Farrelly

Don't Worry about Socrates: Three Plays for Television
Trans. Dan Farrelly

Rules of the Game in Social Relationships
Trans. Dan Farrelly

What Does "Academic" Mean?

Two Essays on the Chances
of the Univeristy Today

JOSEF PIEPER

Translation by Dan Farrelly

ST. AUGUSTINE'S PRESS
South Bend, Indiana

1 2 3 4 5 6   20 19 18 17 16 15

Library of Congress Cataloging in Publication Data
Pieper, Josef, 1904–1997.
[Was heisst akademisch? English]
What does "academic" mean?: two essays on the chances of
the university today / Josef Pieper ;
introduction by James V. Schall; translated by Dan Farrelly.
pages cm
Includes index.
ISBN 978-1-58731-932-7 (hardback: alk paper) —
ISBN 978-1-58731-933-4 (paperbound: alk. paper)
1. Philosophy. 2. Learning and scholarship. I. Title.
B53.P513 2015
001.2 – dc23   2015005660

∞ The paper used in this publication meets the minimu
requirements of the American National Standard for Information
Sciences - Permanence of Paper for Printed Materials,
ANSI Z39.48-1984.

ST. AUGUSTINE'S PRESS
www.staugustine.net

CONTENTS

On What Is Worthy of Our "Veneration"

"Philosophizing is a fundamental attitude to reality which precedes the conscious act and is
largely out of reach of any voluntary disposition
by the *ratio*. In the opinion of the old philosophers it is not at all our decision to grasp a thing
philosophically. If a student came to them saying he wanted to learn how to treat a particular
matter in a philosophic way and was asking
how he should now proceed, the old masters
would likely pose the counter-question: 'Is it in
you, do you as a matter of course normally see
the reality of the world in a certain sense divine
and *therefore worthy of your veneration*—as something which is at least more, and other than, the
mere raw material of human activity?'"

— Josef Pieper, "What Does 'Academic' Mean?"
1950 (17–18)

This short book consists of two Lectures that Josef Pieper
presented at the University of Münster in Germany just
after World War II in 1950. They were later published in
1951, in the journal *Hochland*, but never previously in Eng-
lish. As is ever the case with Pieper, he states the topic
with which he deals frankly and clearly. He recalls its origins, explains what is at stake, and provides a judgment
about its worth. Reading Pieper carefully is itself both a

philosophical act and a distinct pleasure. One always has the sense that he hovers about truth when Pieper is the text before him. No one, except perhaps Aquinas, packs more philosophy and its sources in so few pages as does Josef Pieper. He had a genius for seeing what Hegel, Goethe, Rilke, Augustine, Aristotle, or Plato said and meant. He deftly brings their minds into ours with that sense of our seeing the same truth that they see, a truth that we often miss when reading these authors themselves in their own texts.

On reading this short book, our first reaction will, no doubt, be to wonder if anybody, including ourselves, really obtains a true university education in the modern world. We live in a world filled with people with university degrees from BAs to post-doctoral honors but often with little corresponding universal education. We may know what this thing or that thing is about, but not what the whole world and ourselves in it are about. We do not like to face such issues as they imply that we can discover answers that indicate that we are not ourselves at the origin of *all that is*. In the highest things, we are first receivers, not creators or givers. The world *that is* is fraught with signs of an intelligence that directs itself to our minds, if we would but receive it.

Yet, we are not to despair. All is not lost if someone can recall and re-propose to us just what a university with its education might be. From Plato, we learned that some things, if they are not found in reality, can be located in a mind thinking on this same reality. Josef Pieper is in this tradition. Thus, on seeing the need, it is possible to pose action to attain what the word "academic" ought to mean, that is, a way to think about *what is*. These two essays are directly related to Pieper's earlier and justly famous essays *Leisure: The Basis of Culture* and *The Philosophic Act*. Pieper is ever aware of the relation of freedom to truth. He knows that knowledge and truth exist not in books or abstract forms but in individual human minds and souls actually thinking on *what is*.

In its essence, a university is not an economic or business corporation, nor is it a political institution. It is not a church, a union, or a club. While it has relations to and dealings with all of these otherwise existing institutions of culture and public order, it is itself. It is "set apart" lest the highest things we can know through serious reflection be neglected. Yet, contrary to much popular impression, the university is not hostile to the ordinary life of man. It has its own justification and thus requirements. The word "university" obviously comes from and refers to the notion of *all things that are*. The university is, or ought to be, a place wherein everything can be discussed—not just discussed, but known as true or false. It is widely lamented that under a regime of political correctness, the university is precisely a place where only some things, usually popular or ideological things, are permitted access and funding. When this limitation happens, the university becomes, as it were, an "anti"-university. The university is a dangerous place both because of the power of bad ideas, but also because the truth must not only be known but chosen when known. We are free not to so choose, and such is our doom. This latter possibility is also something that belongs to a university to understand, as any reader of Augustine knows.

Thus, to understand Pieper's concern for the "openness" to all being, we must pay careful attention to the things that are not allowed or likely to be taken under serious consideration. Philosophy, but not sophism, should find a welcome home in the university. Yet, philosophy here, as Pieper points out, does not mean a "department" of philosophy, a survey of philosophers, or "modern" philosophy. Philosophers contradict each other. Rather, philosophy means individuals in every discipline, students and teachers, who think philosophically, who have the habit of confronting what actually *is*. Philosophy is openness to the whole. Many people hold that the purpose of the university is rather "science," or to create jobs. Science in the modern sense, however, is not philosophy. Science in the limited modern sense seeks to know certain definite things about certain existing realities. It has a method that it follows whereby it can find and verify what it discovers. The sciences vary and are distinguished according to the subject matter under investigation. Pieper has no difficulty with such disciplines. But a university is not simply the sum total of the sciences with their own methods.

Pieper often refers to Plato's Academy. He points out that the name itself is an accident, but that it has come to mean what went on in the circle around Socrates. This Academy has some cultic or religious aspect to it. At first sight, in our minds, this aspect will seem to be "anti-philosophic." But for Pieper it is something essential. Its lack in the modern university is a witness to the latter's failure to know what a university really is. Truth is not really protected on the basis of human reason alone. It needs to be aware of the sense of transcendence implicit in every truth that man acknowledges but does not himself make.

Pieper does not oppose "science" to philosophy as if they are intrinsically hostile to each other. But they must be distinguished. To distinguish *what is* and find its causes is the real task of philosophy. The philosopher at his best wants to know what the sciences have come to find out in their respective order. But he also knows that other issues are not brought up in the particular sciences, issues that stand at the core of what man is. Questions come up like "What is death?" "What is freedom?" "Is the world created in justice?" "Am I immortal?" "What is truth?" These issues as such do not belong to any of the particular sciences. They do concern everyone including those who are scientists and their students in their own personal lives.

Pieper sees a certain hierarchy here. That is, all the practical issues do not add up to the issues that most concern us as human beings. If a university is what it says it is by its very name, it should be a place where such questions and answers to them are in the conscious minds of everyone. Moreover, none of these questions can be set aside on the grounds that we have no definite answer to them. What Pieper has in mind with his notion of cult and culture is that reality brings us to these issues with an openness of mind that is willing to listen to all voices that speak or have spoken to us. In this sense, to exclude the responses given by the tradition, by revelation, is to close oneself off from the true nature of human seeking.

The essence of Pieper's thinking on the university is not so much its institutional structure but the condition of the soul of its faculty and students. He simply does not want them to miss out on all that man knows and needs to know about reality, about *what is*. Philosophy exists in conversation and listening. And we can "converse" with Plato and Aristotle, Augustine and Aquinas. We are not restricted to what is happening in the now. If we are so restricted, we are simply not human. Man is the being who remembers. We do not even know what is happening in the "now" if we do not know what happened before us.

The "now" of any age is to be presented to us anew in what a university ought to be.

The question is not one of scheduling of classes or units necessary to graduate. A lack of attention to higher questions means in practice to neglect serious consideration of them. Students leave such universities having been told that they were exposed to everything, to the latest in learning. But they usually find their souls remain empty, that something was missing in a place where everything was said to be taught. One goes away from Pieper with a sense of the wholeness of things. By explaining what philosophy is, he implicitly explains what a university is. The essential justification of a university and its freedom, why it differs from other institutions of culture, is to complete what is not said elsewhere. Man's mind, as Aristotle said and Pieper often repeats, is *capax omnium*. It is that power in us that enables us to know *all that is*. But we are to know freely, because we are free to see the argument, because we can have false arguments corrected in the same freedom. We can also reject what is true, though not without affirming some other partial truth.

Both theology and philosophy ask, not about some particular "specialty," but about the whole. They are the only disciplines that provide this openness to wonder about all things in themselves. This is the wonder that the university should inherit from Aristotle. "But what is peculiar to both philosophy and theology," Pieper writes,

> is precisely that, by their very nature, they are not 'subjects' like other disciplines. Both are, strictly speaking, defined by not being definite, clearly delineated 'special areas.' It could almost be said … that one who philosophizes seriously

is not at all interested in the 'subject' philosophy, just as the theologian, when acting specifically as theologian is not primarily concerned
with 'methodically clean' theology (76).

Not to have a specific subject means to look on all things,
as being, in the case of philosophy, as created by God, in
the case of theology. These two ways of seeing all things
are not contradictory to each other. The "I am who am"
and the "things that are" belong to the same world, the
same truly "open" world, as Pieper would have it.

Pieper notes, in conclusion, that modern scientific
method is aware that there are questions that its approach
cannot deal with. As a result these issues are not considered important, when the very opposite should be at the
center. The issues that can be answered are relatively uninteresting. Once we know how to build a mousetrap, the
knowledge is no longer an adventure, though it is useful
and good. It is the maddening fact that there are things
that we cannot fully answer that is most challenging to us,
that most alerts us to that mystery of things still to be ac-
counted for. "That which makes a university to be a university," Pieper writes, "cannot be discovered by a mere
factual description but by the attempt to have sight of the
invisible existential experiences which have been absorbed into the institution of the university" (67). A university is a university only when its students and faculty
are brought to the same existential experiences that bring
man to his fullness in his contemplation of the truth of
things and their origins. The teacher and the student both
contemplate the same reality that alone decides *what is*.
This is why truth is, in principle, free.

There is no such thing as a university in which the

reading of Plato is not going on in the souls of its students. Academia is the inheritance of Plato. In all of university life, there is still nothing like the reading of Plato, the reading him together, student and professor, or if the professor or student will not read, to read him by ourselves. When we come to Plato, as Pieper so often teaches, we come to the *Laws*; we come to the realization of the "unseriousness of human affairs," as I like to call it.[1] It will seem paradoxical to suggest that our affairs are not serious or important. But Plato's point is that God is what is really serious; the pursuit of all else, while fascinating, pales by comparison.

In Pieper's view, a university is a principled place, though not the only place, where the pursuit of *what is* takes place, or ought to take place. It is a place where we seek to know the whole in an openness that includes both reality and what is handed down to us. The proper end of knowledge is truth and the proper end of knowing it is festivity, something that can only be a free response to the joy caused in us when we realize that reality is not a necessity but a gift for us to know, a gift to set us free to rejoice also in what is not ourselves.

---

1   See James V. Schall, *The Unseriousness of Human Affairs* (Wilmington: ISI Books, 2001).

WHAT DOES "ACADEMIC" MEAN?*

*   This text, originally written for a lecture held in the context of International Holiday Courses at the University of Münster (1950), was published in the periodical *Hochland* (Munich), no. 43, June 1951.

A Western Concept

The name used by the Athenian, in the fourth century BC, when he wanted to give a name to Plato's school—the building, the garden and the community of those learning and philosophising there—this name, "Academy," was settled on by chance. It is a purely external designation which has nothing to do with the essence of the school, let alone saying anything about its essence. Everyone knows that the reason for, and the origin of, the name lay in the purely spatial proximity of the school to the grove of an Athenian City Hero (*Akádemos*).

So one should perhaps ask whether our word "academy," this generic name deriving from the original proper name, is based—just like the designation "academic"—on a chance, external correspondence between our schools and Plato's school at the grove of Akádemos. That would be nothing unusual. There is no lack of such inconsequential, purely verbal links with antiquity. We speak quite freely of Jupiter lamps and Apollo light plays without anyone asking whether there is any intrinsic link with the gods of antiquity. Or—and this is an obvious example—no one will seriously want to see in the name "Lyceum" a specific and binding link between our schools for senior girls and Aristotle's research and teaching community, the Lýkeion.

Again: do the word and the concept "academic" bear any other relation to antiquity than this chance, external reference occurring in ordinary parlance? If not, what would be the sense of discussing the question "What does academic mean?" in relation to Plato? The question would be exposed to the vagaries of a given time and place. It would also be completely uninteresting. Above all, in this case it would be meaningless to discuss it from the point of view of the Western tradition; yet the concept "academic" is, in a special sense, a truly Western concept.

To begin with, one can say with some justification that there is a factual and historical continuity between our universities and Plato's original academy from which everything academic in the world takes its name. Even here there is something special. It is not enough to trace the modern university back to the universities of the medieval period, which are themselves inconceivable without the model of the East Roman and Byzantine education system.[1] It is immediately prior to the emergence of the first universities in the West that, in Byzantium, the Imperial University was restored by Emperor Constantine Monomachos. But this act was only a rebirth of something that had long since existed, namely *the* Imperial Academy which, under this name, had been founded six hundred years previously (425) by Theodosius II—and indeed more or less explicitly as a daughter foundation of, but also in opposition to, the school of Plato which was still in existence— identical with his school —in Athens. However, the person to whom this first Christian university owes its intellectual origin is an Athenian woman, the daughter of a philosopher and her-

---

1.   See H. Rashdall, The Universities of Europe in the Middle Ages. Edited by F. M. Powicke and A. B. Emden (Oxford 1936), vol. 1, pp. 79, 358, 505. Also Otto Immisch, Academia (Freiburg i. Br. 1924).

self highly educated in philosophy and the arts. She was probably a pupil and initiate of Plato's Academy itself and of its director, Plutarch of Athens. She was a woman who, through one of life's adventures, came to the Imperial throne in Byzantium as the wife of Theodosius: Empress Eudocia, who before her baptism was called Athenaïs.[2] The work of the magician Cyprianus, described as the first version of the Faust material, is traceable back to the same Eudocia. It is quite amazing how the strands of tradition are linked here, among them one—though not the only one—associating Plato's school with the educational institutions, which, down to the present, call themselves "academic."

More important than this factual and historical continuity is the other point: Plato's school has continuously been understood and designated as an essential guideline and basic model for our universities. "Platonissare" and "academicum se facere" means, in the parlance of the humanists, much the same thing.[3] But it is not as if Plato was "rediscovered" only at the beginning of the modern era. Not only is the dominant figure of the medieval period the Platonist Augustine who again and again conceived of his "schools"—far removed from the world—as akin to the garden in the grove of *Akádemos*. There is also, of course, the fact, somewhat neglected by historians, that the medieval universities, especially Paris, were understood by contemporaries as the fruit of a *translatio studii*— i.e., a process of tradition, by virtue of which the "Study

2.   Ferdinand Gregorovius, Athenaïs. Geschichte einer Byzantinischen Kaiserin. Printed in: Ferdinand Gregorovius, Athen und Athenaïs (Dresden 1927), p. 767f.
3.   Fritz Halbhauer, Mutianus Rufus und seine geistesgeschichtliche Stellung (Leipzig-Berlin 1929), p. 101f.

of Wisdom" was transmitted from Athens via Rome to the Franks.[4]

In the above, some of the reasons may have become clear as to why, in all languages among peoples of the Occident, this word "academic" can designate, down to the present, a norm and a claim, the meaning of which, it seems, cannot be fully obliterated unless the intellectual substance of the West is itself destroyed. Of course, this possibility has in our age, for the first time, become visible as an acute danger—and by no means only one which threatens from outside. This gives the question "What does academic mean?" a new significance. It involves issues which are both current and almost political. It goes beyond the "purely academic" and leaves it way behind.

4. E. Gilson has devoted an enlightening essay to this theme of the translation studii ("un thème littéraire trop négligé"): L'humanisme médieval. Printed in: Les idées et les lettres (Paris 1932), pp. 132–85.

Philosophical means theoretical

Whoever asks, "What does academic mean?"—not as someone interested in the historic aspect but as one concerned with the present situation—whoever asks, over and above the information provided by social statistics, what is essential and distinctive about the "academic," such a person is necessarily referred back to Plato's school.

That can, of course, not mean that the concrete manifestation of current academic education would have to be recognizable in an historically concrete manifestation of Plato's Academy, or vice versa. But it does mean that what gives Plato's school its intrinsic form is also the inner form-principle of our academic institutions. At least, so it would have to be, if the term "academic" could be applied to them with justification.

This is to say something quite fundamental, and also quite positive, for whatever idea we might have of the teaching, the curriculum and material taught in Plato's school (there is a whole spectrum of opinions about these matters), one indisputable fact is that Plato's school in Athens was a *philosophical* school, a community of people philosophising, so that its intrinsic characteristic is philosophy, the philosophical way of looking at the world. From this, as a first defining element of the academic, results the thesis: academic means philosophical; an academic educational institution is a philosophical one – one which is at least based on philosophy. To pursue a branch of knowledge in an academic way means to pursue it philosophically. And consequently, an education that is not philosophically based and not shaped on philosophical principles cannot properly be called academic. A subject of study that has no philosophical orientation is not academic.

Naturally, we now have to ask: What does philosophical mean?—and the answer will have to be pondered with an eye to Plato.

The term "philosophical" by no means refers to a corpus of teachings or propositions, but rather to a way of looking at life.[1] This, of course, can be named and defined as something distinct. It is a way of seeing things which has always been described as *theoretical*: "philosophical" amounts to "theoretical." At first sight this seems quite banal and somewhat insipid, but the statement takes on a very critical and aggressive meaning as soon as it is understood in its exact sense. What, namely, is the original meaning of "theoretical" and "*theoria*?" What is meant is an attitude towards the world which is only concerned with the fact that things reveal themselves as they are— which is what truth actually consists of. To be aiming at truth and nothing else is the essence of *theoria*, as Aristotle says in his *Metaphysics*[2]—in which he is of one mind with his teacher Plato; and the medieval commentator, Thomas Aquinas, is entirely in agreement. The aim of theoretical knowledge is truth, whereas the aim of practical knowledge is the achieving of targets. And even if the *practici* aim at knowing truth in relation to particular things, truth

1.   Otto Seel has misunderstood this point, just as, in a discussion of the first edition of this book, he has unbelievably misinterpreted a number of things. See Otto Seel, Die platonische Akademie (Stuttgart 1953), p. 39f.
2.   Metaphysics 993 b.

is still not their primary aim. They gear truth to practice. But philosophy, and above all the philosophical doctrine of being, metaphysics—the most philosophical discipline—is pre-eminently a *scientia veritatis*,[3] *theoria* in the fullest sense. That is the teaching common to Plato, Aristotle, and Thomas; it is simply the teaching of the "ancients."

To look at a thing philosophically, to look at a reality in a philosophical way, would therefore mean explicitly prescinding from all that we normally call "practical life" and "accomplishing real tasks" (expressions which implicitly seem to imply that "mere" knowledge of truth is of itself *not* a "real" task).

In the old definition of philosophising as a purely theoretical attitude to the world, the approach that characterises modern philosophy is not taken into account. I am referring to the power aspect of knowledge, the *potentia humana*, with which Bacon's *Novum organum* identifies true knowledge.[4] He is referring to orientation towards practicality, applicability, usefulness. He means that the goal is a practical philosophy which puts us in a position to become *maîtres et possesseurs de la nature*.[5] From the perspective of the old concept of philosophy this Bacon-Descartes approach is unphilosophical, because it affects the purity of *theoria* and even destroys it.

But such insistence on the theoretical character of philosophy is not only "unmodern"; rather, the challenge involved in it is timeless. After all, it is not purely by chance

3. Thomas Aquinas, Commentary to Aristotle's Metaphysics 2, 2; no. 290.
4. I, 3.
5. Descartes, Discours de la Méthode, cap. 6.

that Western history of philosophy begins with the laughter of a Thracian maid who sees the philosopher fall into a well as he contemplates the heavens. Plato's comment on this in the *Theaetetus* is that both this laughter and the cause of it can scarcely be done away with; "again and again" the philosopher will be laughed at, not only by Thracian maids but also by "the many" because, being not of this world, he stumbles into wells and also into many other embarrassments.[6]

So the quality of seeming to "the many" to be an oddity, the separation from the activity of everyday life, the otherworldliness as a constant feature of genuine philosophising—these would not be understood as due to chance but as belonging to the essence of the thing itself—because philosophical is the same as theoretical (i.e., not practical).

This formulation is, of course, a conscious exaggeration which is open to misunderstanding, but I believe that it expresses what is central to the meaning of "philosophical" and "academic." It does so with much greater precision than all the attempts to base the inner justification of academic education on its "importance for life" or on its importance for technical, economic, or military praxis – or for any other kind of praxis. It is not possible, I believe, to defend the academic character of the university by saying that it is not really all that academic. Working with the original concept of the "academic" one sees the absurdity to which all of the above attempts lead. If the academic is defended in such ways—where practicality is the decisive factor—the inner core of the academic which one thinks or claims one is protecting is instead surrendered. One has

6.   Plato, Theaetetus, 174 c.

already joined forces with the Thracian maid and "the many."

Let us sum up the foregoing with two points. First point: if the term "academic" is more than a purely external designation its original meaning must be the same as "philosophical." On the basis of this origin, academic education amounts to philosophical education; the academic character of university study would be seen in the fact that the individual disciplines would be studied in a philosophical way. Second point: "philosophical" means "theoretical." This does not mean that the concept of the philosophical is thereby exhaustively defined, but that a very essential characteristic is indicated. Wherever there is philosophical questioning, a reality is focused on in a receptive, knowing process; and this receptive grasp of reality (which is itself a high form of activity and realisation[7]) comes about without an eye to the "power" associated with such knowledge and without judging its applicability and relevance for some kind of "praxis" or other. So, does this turning away from everything that one calls "practical importance" form part of the essence of the academic?

7.   With reference to the contrast between theoria and praxis it is *not*, as Seel interprets it (Platonische Akademie pp. 45f.), an "antithesis between seeing and doing" but a distinction between knowing truth on the one hand and achieving utilitarian goals on the other. But even this latter, of course, has its place and is necessary. There can be no question of attributing "absolute and exclusive rights to theory" (ibid. p. 48) or of a "rigorous bracketing of the practicable" (ibid. p.54).

Destruction through being pressed into service

It is now time to introduce a question mark and to give voice to some objections which have probably been waiting a long time to be heard.

Is it not absurd to define the academic by limiting it to the philosophical/theoretical as we have done? After all, does not every university student take on a particular career in which the knowledge gained can be fruitfully applied? And is not the point of this study precisely to train good doctors, chemists, lawyers? How can it be un-academic to concern oneself with setting such goals? Furthermore: concretely, what would the study of a subject—say, chemistry—look like when carried out "in a philosophical way"?

In reply to the first objection: of course our universities are institutions of professional training, which was certainly not the case with Plato's school in the grove of Akádemos. This is, admittedly, a non-academic element of modern, but also of medieval universities. Yet universities still, at least in Germany, claim to be *more* than mere professional training institutions.[1] But how can this claim be justified, and what does this "more" consist of if one leaves aside the academic/philosophical?

The meaning of the claim cannot be reduced to saying that the sphere of the academic exists *side by side* with the

1. See, for example, the Hamburg "Gutachten zur Hochschulreform," Introduction, section B, 3.

sphere of the actual professional training. What is meant is that professional training in the true university is *itself* academic. The academic conditions the character of the professional training as professional training.

Objection: and so it is not contradictory to the essence of the academic to be concerned with practical goals?—A reply to this is not easy to formulate. The relationship between *theoria* and the usefulness of what results from it is not easy to grasp. "Expressly to want something not to happen" and "not expressly to want something to happen" are, as we know, two different things. But there are other goals in human experience which *cannot* be reached when one explicitly aims at them. There are things of value that come into our possession only as an "extra"—as the fruit, so to speak, of our seeking something else. "Anyone who tries to preserve his life will lose it; and anyone who loses it will keep it safe" (Luke 17, 33): these biblical words are far from being a purely rhetorical antithesis. They express a real content—one, which, by no means limited to the religious sphere, cannot be communicated with precision in any other than this contradictory form.

Applied to our subject it would mean: of course the professional excellence of the doctor, the scientist and the lawyer is a highly desirable fruit of academic study. But could it not be that such excellence, once it rises above the level of the mediocre and of purely technical learning, is linked to and conditioned by selfless, purely theoretical and receptive absorption into being—without regard to success? Could it not be that the practical usefulness depends precisely on whether the *theoria* has previously been realised in its purity? This is by no means an unrealistic, romantic exaggeration. There is a lot to be said for the argument that, quite generally, research deprived of a foundation in pure *theoria*—of "academic" character—(for example, if the rationalised planning to achieve goals in the context of an absolutely work-oriented state were radically to destroy the theoretical/academic element) would thereby become sterile; this means that it would precisely not produce the useful effect although (no: because) this useful effect has been desired exclusively and "absolutely."

This has already partly answered the second question: how does a discipline studied in "a philosophical way" differ concretely and clearly from one studied in a non-philosophical way? The distinction is to be sought in this "purely theoretical" character of the approach to the subject: the decisive factor is the special way of looking into the depth of things so that they are no longer seen as these so-and-so definable things and their usefulness for that-and-that purpose, but as forms of the most amazing imaginable reality: namely, as forms of being. It is this moving out of our enclosed narrow environment—with all its rigidly defined aspects—into the open universe of total reality where we encounter being as being. It is the astonishment experienced, as penetrating research presses forward and is confronted with the unfathomable depths of the world—i.e., confronted with the mysterious character of being itself; confronted with the mystery found in the fact that something "is." It is the forgetting, above all, of direct goals in life—a forgetting which happens (for better or for worse?) to the person experiencing this astonishment. All of this is therefore what distinguishes the inner structure, the attitude, the atmosphere that obtains in the study of a specific discipline carried out in a philosophical way. The decisive element is the freedom from being bound to any kind of utilitarian goals. This freedom is genuine "academic freedom," which *per definitionem* is destroyed as soon as the disciplines merely serve to achieve the targets set by large, powerful concerns no matter how these are organised.

In the term "academic freedom" the word "academic" can be substituted by "philosophical." Individual disciplines can indeed be used to serve utilitarian ends. This is not repugnant to the essence of a particular discipline. Concretely: a government can very well say that it needs, for carrying out a five-year plan, physicists who in this or that particular respect can catch up with progress made in other countries; or, we need scholars in medicine to produce a more effective remedy against influenza. This can be said and done without prejudice to the essence of the individual discipline. *But:* we need philosophers to develop, establish and defend a particular ideology—this cannot be said without thereby destroying philosophy. There *can* only be philosophical *theoria* where it is free. Here we are not talking about the logical or psychological incompatibility of *theoria* on the one hand and, on the other hand, service of utilitarian goals. No: this connection is, in reality, lethal. Philosophical *theoria* is destroyed by being pressed into service. One can think one is *using* philosophy, but insofar as one does it is no longer philosophy. Philosophy is free or it is not philosophy. Individual disciplines, on the other hand, can only be free to the extent that they are carried out in an academic way—i.e., with philosophical *theoria*. (By freedom—it should be stressed here again—is merely meant independence of orientation to utilitarian goals. Obviously what is not meant is that philosophy can be free from the tie to objective truth. But the realisation of this tie presupposes that freedom.[2])

2. See Josef Pieper, Was heißt Philosophieren?, 5th edition (Munich 1963), p. 31.

Of course, the difference—in fact and in principle—between an academic/philosophical and a non-philosophical engagement in professional study has become very nearly imperceptible. Precisely this is characteristic of our intellectual situation: the distinctive—and that means the essential—point of the academic can hardly be isolated any more. One would have to ask the question: how does the chemistry department of a university differ from that of a modern medical concern? It is to be feared that for the most part the difference could not be defined. (Perhaps one might think that the only difference is that the industrial setups are better equipped and better financed than the academic!) But that would mean that the difference between the academic and the non-academic, and consequently also the meaning of academic *freedom*, could no longer be known—a state of affairs which we indeed seem to be approaching.

This state of affairs can be seen in suggestions for reform: for example, that the academic character of university study can be rescued or restored by adding more general studies to any particular individual professional subject.[3] A *studium generale* of this kind is undoubtedly desirable, but one cannot expect to base the academic character of the university on it. The academic character of the university can only be constituted by having all disciplines—even the individual ones, and precisely these—treated in an academic, and therefore philosophical way. Through the mere addition of subject areas—even the subject "philosophy"—not much can be changed (not to speak of the other subjects which have also been suggested, of a generally educational kind, such as sociology

3.   See Hamburg "Gutachten," section "Studium Generale."

or even economics!⁴) All this, quite apart from the fact that even philosophy as a subject can be studied in a very unphilosophical way. It is not through philosophy as a subject amongst other subjects that a study achieves the inner character of the academic, but philosophy as a principle, as a *modus* of contemplation, as a basic attitude to the world. And one could almost say that even the study of philosophy (as a subject) can conversely profit from the study of individual disciplines *insofar as* these are carried out in a philosophical way. Given this presupposition, even a much greater degree of "specialization" could be accepted without harm. On the supposition that individual disciplines be studied in the philosophical way, the very thing which, in uncustomary agreement, has long been seen as the real danger would now be acceptable.

4.   Ibid.

"The exclusive property of the gods"

The philosophical, taken in such an old sense, lives, of course, from a hidden root of which we now need to speak. The concept of the academic will also be seen to be more profound than was first suspected.

We have become accustomed to say and to think that we could, if we wanted, look at a thing from various angles: the historical, the psychological, the sociological—and even from the philosophical standpoint. Such a way of speaking, which is something we are completely familiar with and take for granted, is based on the opinion that we can "apply" the philosophical perspective, that we can occupy or relinquish the philosophical standpoint, that nothing but a mental operation is required to set in motion a philosophical consideration of the subject. But Plato, Aristotle, Augustine and Thomas have considered this opinion to be completely inadequate. For them, philosophising is a fundamental attitude to reality which precedes the conscious act and is largely out of reach of any voluntary disposition by the *ratio*. In the opinion of the old philosophers it is not at all our decision to grasp a thing philosophically. If a student came to them saying he wanted to learn how to treat a particular matter in a philosophical way and was asking how he should now proceed, the old masters would be likely to pose the counter question: "Is it in you, do you as a matter of course normally see the reality of the world as in a certain sense divine and therefore worthy of your veneration—as something which is at least more, and other than, the mere raw material of human activity?" If we were privy to such a conversation it would not be easy for us to find out what this question might have to do with philosophy. But it does very precisely concern the possibility of philosophical *theoria*. Why? Because it is intrinsically incomprehensible; because we simply cannot manage to contemplate purely theoretically, in the fullest sense of the word—and that means philosophically—a world which is exclusively or primarily looked on as material for our use. There can only be *theoria* in the full sense, and it can only be achievable as an attitude, where the world is seen as having a meaning based on a higher than human authority.

If we now remind ourselves that the concepts theoretical/philosophical/academic belong intrinsically together and that, furthermore, academic freedom is nothing but the freedom of *theoria* from service and setting of targets in the world of praxis, then it becomes evident that the whole sphere of what constitutes the academic, and above all the freedom related to it, rests on a foundation one would not expect, and that this freedom—without its foundation—has no roots and cannot survive.

We are perhaps inclined to see these issues as mere "intellectual history" (Geistesgeschichte) and not as something "real." With regard to scientific freedom, we consider that we know from experience that it is threatened not so much by the loss of its metaphysical foundations as by very real forces. Precisely these very real forces are reckoned with in the original conception of the academic. The structure of the Platonic Academy seems to reflect this insight: that the free realm constituted by *theoria* cannot avoid being sucked up into the possession of daimonic powers which strive to turn all reality into raw material for their utilitarian plans. Freedom of *theoria* is defense-less—*unless it puts itself in a special way under the protection of the gods.* This elementary craving for the utilitarian feeds off basic needs and is legitimised by them. This is all the more so when it is allied to political power or when it is identical with the will of the political power itself. This utilitarian will is, as it were, by its very nature so inclined to absolutize itself and to reduce everything—including man and his highest powers—to an instrument (even if this turns out to be no longer "useful" at all) that the attempt to remove a particular sphere in principle from the utilitarian must seem hopeless from the start—unless this sphere is withdrawn from the utilitarian in such a way that it, as the old Roman formulation says, is made "into the exclusive property of the gods."[1] But this is precisely what happens in Plato's Academy: it was, amongst other things, in the strict sense a ritualistic society, a *thiasos*, a society which gathered at particular times for ritual celebration and for offering sacrifices! (There was even an officer for preparing sacrifices.[2])

We know very little accurate detail, and it would in any case go beyond the framework of our present task, to examine, for example, whether Plato owes the idea of such a community—like that of a religious order—to the Pythagorean schools in Sicily and southern Italy (which is probable); or which god is the object of the Academy's cult. The muses are named, but we know very little about the theological status of the muses. Plato himself calls

---

1. Reallexikon für Antike und Christentum (Leipzig 1942), article "Arbeitsruhe," column 590.
2. See Hermann Usener, Organisation der wissenschaftlichen Arbeit, in: Vorträge und Aufsätze (Leipzig-Berlin 1914), pp. 76ff.

them (in *Laws*) the festival companions which the gods have given to the human race, born to hardship, for the recurring cultic feast days.[3] One may understand the muses, as Plato does Eros,[4] as daimonic middle beings between god and man or as lower deities—in any case, they are *real* forces in the religious sphere. Modern notions of "serving the muses," "temple of the muses," "sanctuary of art and science" reflect a "fantastic" imitation arising from fantasy (Goethe's words[5]). They are a sham reality. A genuine correspondence, on the other hand—if one is to be named—would be angelic powers and the liturgical space.[6] The factual and legal freedom of Plato's Academy therefore corresponded to inner freedom and found its most extreme realisation in the liturgical act. This act, of itself and prior to every legal initiative, is what, through the force of rapture, gives the person inner freedom and releases him from the ties to fulfilling direct goals in life. In this way the sphere of freedom in fact and in law is made possible and is constituted from within—it is the freedom of the *scholé* and of leisure in one.[7]

It would be to underestimate the profound meaning of the Western concept of the academic, and especially of academic freedom, if one were to separate it from its origins—which are by no means reducible to external facts, but which remain internal and fruitful and are able to remain effective even when political force (not because it honors "other" gods but because it honors no gods at all!).

3. Laws 653 d.
4. Symposium 202 e.
5. Goethe to Riemer 26 March 1814.
6. See Josef Pieper, Muße und Kult, 6th edition (Munich 1961), pp. 84ff.
7. Ibid. pp. 14f.

has set aside the inviolable rights of that realm of freedom in the academic sphere as "liberal nonsense." Even if the academic as an institution were no longer to have any public existence, it would still be able to realise itself in the innermost enclave of contemplation: as the attitude of *theoria* which becomes aware of being and reveres it. The freedom of *theoria* would have to prove itself by its opposition: although without weapons, giving witness to the truth.

This represents both a cardinal aspect of the concept "academic" and a cardinal answer to the question: what does academic mean?

The "worker" and the sophist

The task remains to give – through the use of some counter images and contrasts—a sharper focus to what we have outlined. We will be speaking of one form in which the academic is simply and explicitly *negated* and of another more dangerous form in which it is deceptively *affirmed*. The first is that of the *functionary* and the second that of the *sophist*.

If we are now to speak first of the functionary or—in a still more dangerous formulation—of the "worker" as of someone diametrically opposed to the essence of the academic, misunderstanding is carefully to be avoided from the start. But in my experience it has often seemed to be unavoidable. It is as if we were dealing here with a *social* definition and a hiving off of the academic. It is not the social stratum made up of workers or normal people as a whole who are seen here as the counterpart to the academic and as excluded from this sphere. We are, on the contrary, convinced that the normal person—as long as he is conscious of his normality (something which depends on the circumstances)—has his own approach to thinking about and "celebrating" the world as a whole. In this, the best and most genuine part of the academic attitude is also realised.

But what do we mean by worker and functionary if not the working man? In the first number of the first annual edition of *Frankfurter Hefte*[1] it is stated that the new

---

1.   April number 1946, p. 8.

}23{

university will have to be characterised not just by its being open to the gifted worker but much more by the students being "workers even though they do not come from the working class." One will, of course, take for granted the first part of the requirement. But what is meant by the "worker" which the student, without being a worker, must be? Here the distinction is made between the worker as a reality, as belonging to a real group within society, and the worker as—well, what? As an ideal abstraction, a quasi moral quality (the way one speaks of a "praying" person or a "fighter"). It is not as if this worker model has not been concretely realised. But the sphere in which it is realised is not identical with the social class of the manual worker. It is not possible to define the degree of elevation above the work and income situation of this social class that is needed if I am to know clearly whether someone is a "worker" in the sense of that abstract ideal. But this latter is precisely the worker— and the only one—we are dealing with here as the contrast to the academic.

But what does this "worker" model involve? It is the condition in which life is defined by "service," the complete integration of the person as part of the machinery of comprehensive planning. This idea of the "worker" becomes really interesting when we see the emotional vehemence—even religious fervour—with which the "transformation of the individual into a worker"[2] is usually affirmed and proclaimed by the fascinated believers. Not only does total identification with function seem to be the essence of the new human nobility; not only is expressly the element of uniform and mask, expressly the

2. Ernst Jünger, Blätter und Steine (Hamburg 1934), p. 175.

"soullessness" of the functionary's face[3]—as if carved out of metal or special kinds of wood—praised as the exemplary form taken on by the new man. Not only that. No. Ernst Jünger, whose formulations we have used here, speaks (or: spoke) of the individual coming to the point where, having taken on this work characteristic, "he can, without hesitation, be sacrificed";[4] he spoke of the "cult level"[5] of this process of "construction" and "toughening" of "planning landscapes"—the achieving of which is the "historical task" of the worker.

In its historical process every heresy goes through the phase of the heroic. In this phase its energy and fascination reach a climax. It is difficult to say whether this climax of the heretical absolutising of the "functionary" has already been reached. It seems that it has not. Above all, no one will seriously believe that fascination with the "worker" model has remained limited to the totalitarian regimes and that it fell away when they did. The ideal of the "heroic pure functionary" seems to exercise its power precisely over an elite of young students. Of course, in a virtually daimonic way it is combined with another very legitimate ideal which is born of necessity and makes of this necessity a virtue. I am referring to the ideal of an ascetically disciplined meagre existence which then erroneously takes itself to be, and calls itself, "proletarian."

There is no need to say that the philosophical attitude of *theoria* on the one hand and, on the other hand, the attitude of carrying out the absolute requirements for the

---

3. Ibid. p. 207; see also "Der Arbeiter," 2nd edition (Hamburg 1933), p. 116ff.
4. Blätter und Steine, p. 211.
5. Ibid. p. 133.

fulfilment of some goal or other are quite mutually exclusive. The worker model depends on the idea that the satisfaction of needs is glorified by symbols of the heroic and elevated to the metaphysical level of a salvation process. But "academic" (= philosophical-theoretical) says precisely that the true, genuine wealth of man does *not* lie in his being *maître et possesseur de la nature*, and not at all in any kind of "competence" (all of which is not only important for life but even *necessary*!). Instead the ultimate and genuine wealth of man—that which makes it worthwhile to be human—is his ability to grasp what is; his ability to be conscious of being itself and of things themselves not just as beneficial or harmful, useful or useless, but as being. The wealth of man is based on the fact that, receptive and aware, he is *capax universi*, capable of coming into contact with the totality of what is—*convenire cum omni ente*.[6]

The incompatibility of the academic with the model of the "worker" is thus clear. But it is likewise clear that, pouring into this latter position—which stands in opposition to the academic—are elemental factors which really belong to the sacred sphere but are no longer in use there. It is true, though, that the shape this model takes in everyday life operates less through fascination than through the massive claim that all human activity has to serve public utilitarian needs, production, and progress. It is clear that the might of this contrary model cannot be overcome by the force of humanist education, not by the "merely academic," but—if it can happen at all—by the original force of the academic which has to be won back: namely, by the rapturous force of a philosophical *theoria* which conjures up our true wealth and is open to the *mirandum* of creation.

6. Thomas Aquinas, Quaest. disp. de veritate I, I.

Purely humanistic education, divorced from this origin, is what makes for the sophist—this and some other factors.

The sophist is a timeless figure, and the battle fought by Socrates-Plato against Protagoras and Gorgias is never-ending. It will have to be continued by anyone who calls on the authority of Plato's school, the Academy, which was an anti-sophist institution.

But what is, more precisely, a sophist? There is a variety of manifestations. There is the relativist Protagoras who was the first to formulate the fundamental principle of every form of sophistic humanism: that man is the measure of all things. There is the bewildering Hippias who knew everything. There is Prodicos, who is able to explain the loftiest things in the most common terms, showing up greatness as hiding its all-too-human qualities, so that "genuine" reality is identified as the average. Nothing in the world deserves respect. Then there is, above all, Gorgias, the nihilist who charms with his formal elegance. He surrounds the *nihil* with the dazzling linguistic charm of *haute littérature*. He achieves precisely that "blunting of the mind by brilliance" of which Goethe spoke.[7] What all of these particular forms of sophistry have in common is exactly that which separates them from the striving after knowledge which has its greatest witnesses in Socrates and Plato. It is the striving, identical down through the centuries, to discover the foundation of reality and of existence. That man can attain to his real spiritual possessions only in an attitude of silent *theoria*—concerning himself with truth and nothing else, like a

---

7. Maximen und Reflexionen. Kröners Taschenausgabe, edited by Günther Müller, no. 944.

listener *receiving* his way of measuring things from the reality of the world which has been there before him—this is something the sophist will never accept. He will reject even more the idea that there could be such a thing as "sacred tradition," based on a message about the world and existence as a whole, from a higher than human source which also sustains the message. He chooses freedom—however empty it is—and achieves it by forgetting long established wisdom. Commitment to "tradition" seems to the critical autonomous subject to be unjustified and, above all, unbearable. And as far as the spirit's deeper, prior, more essential commitment to the norm of objective being is concerned, the sophist dissolves this link because for him content is unimportant compared with the purely formal.

Perhaps the sophist does not sense that this very twofold lack of commitment is what makes him prone to, and "ripe" for, becoming the instrument of totalitarian powers. Anyone who refuses to accept truth as a norm is enabling, even provoking and promoting commitment to inappropriate goals, to the arbitrarily chosen targets of some type of praxis. Perhaps the sophist does not realise that, on his way, he could encounter the figure of the "worker"; and perhaps he would not like this encounter. But that does not alter the fact that this link between the two deviant forms of relationship to the truth in fact exists and is in reality (one would be inclined to say: in *political reality*) becoming established. For example, the humanities influenced by sophistry can not only not slow down or reverse the decline of academic freedom but can even accelerate it.

But here we can say somewhat more exactly how this sophist degeneration of the academic is manifested in the concrete. First, the mere piling up of information and knowledge—already much disparaged, by the way—is more important to the polymath Hippias than to the founder of the Academy and cannot be considered academic. Second, there is the more debatable question of whether the scientifically systematic knowledge of a closed individual discipline is *eo ipso* to be designated as academic in the original sense. One would surely have to say that a person who is a subject specialist can only be considered an academic if, and insofar as, he sees the object of his study not merely as this particular object but also as "a being as such." But this would mean going beyond the discipline, in such a way that the horizon of total reality—i.e., the philosophical dimension—would be entered. Third, a completely sophistic and therefore unacademic figure would be the person whose "education" is in pure form, with only an aesthetic and literary culture, the "writer" (in the sense of Confucius, that a person for whom form outweighs content is a writer); "rhetoric" in this sense is the real domain of the sophists, who, as Plato said, are in no way inclined to call a man a "powerful speaker" just because he speaks the truth.[8]

But this is all more or less harmless. Knowing everything, isolated knowledge of a particular discipline, lack of commitment in literature, formalist lack of content—these forms of degeneration do not constitute the most extreme contrast to the essence of the academic. We still have to name this extreme contrast, in which the truly academic is actually betrayed—indeed behind the mask of the academic itself. But this is to be said of every institution dedicated to scientific teaching and learning which is

8. Apologia 17 b 4 f.

expressly *not rooted in revering reality*—the revering, above all, of being itself which Plato[9] called the criterion of philosophising. Wherever the "critical" element is so much in force that it makes the revering attitude simply impossible, there we have the most extreme form of anti-academic sophistry, which, despite a perhaps extreme formal perfection, destroys the core of the academic. In referring to "criticism" we are naturally not thinking of the incorruptibility of thinking based on evidence but of that arrogant and smug attitude that refuses to be taught and appears in a variety of forms—for example, in the form of seeming indifference towards the reality that deserves our profound respect, and this in the guise of "objectivity"; or, with more acerbity and aggression, in the attitude of denunciation on principle—an attitude of wanting only to unmask. Or, as in some forms of existentialist nihilism, as sheer cynicism that takes nothing seriously outside of itself.

But why is the substance of the academic affected when the reverential attitude is gone? Because without it the *theoria* in its full and undiluted sense cannot function. This *theoria* is the silently receptive awareness of reality, in which what is crucial in the philosophical act takes place—the act which, again, constitutes the essence of the academic.

This closes the circle of our discussion: in the concept of *theoria*, the inner possibility of which is destroyed by the sophist, and which, when realised concretely, must run counter to any kind of utilitarian plans of the "worker." Both, therefore, sophist and "worker," show that they are indeed *the* typical antitheses of the academic.

9.   Politeia 480 a.

Separation from "the many"

Just one further comment: a new theme—quite separate, a "coda"—in the shape of a question which I am unable to answer.

In Plato's dialog *Theaetetus* the "Tracian maid", with her realistic laughter, stands expressly for "the many."[1] This can only mean that in Plato's opinion the opponent of the philosophiser and of the philosophical stance is none other than the average person living an everyday practical existence—the majority, the crowd, the mass of people. Not only is the realisation of the philosophical *theoria* not something for the many but that this realisation takes place in spite of them. It is in the nature of things that philosophising is unpopular (in both senses of the word: not comprehensible, and not liked). To them it is foreign, suspect, and laughable.

The question posed here is the following: does it belong to the essence of the academic to be expressly separated from the many? And what would this involve?

If we consider the explosive problems currently associated with the controversial term "democracy" it is clear what a minefield we are moving in. But that should not dispense us from dealing directly with the question—and cautiously take into account that the answer, in the great tradition of the West is: yes, the academic sphere is essentially marked off from the many!

1.   174 c.

That is the reason for Plato's aversion to the written word: that it is not able to be silent to people when it would be better to be silent to them.[2] This is not based on an *a priori* decision, a question of principle. Instead, it is a judgement based on experience—of course, very fundamental human experience; perhaps one could say: experience of human nature. "What more beautiful thing could we have done in life than to shed light on the essence of things for *everyone*!"—that is what Plato exclaimed as an old man (seventh letter); but he adds resignedly: in his opinion it is not possible to speak or write adequately for the many.[3]

When, in *Politics*,[4] Aristotle says with regard to the "common attraction" of certain forms of music that "the great crowd of slaves" is receptive to it, he means "the many," and it would be wrong to interpret the concept of "slave" as akin to what needs to be overcome by the "abolition of slavery" or by social progress. Even the Christian Thomas Aquinas speaks of the "foolish throng" (*multitudo stultorum*) that chases after money and does not realise that wisdom cannot be bought.[5]

Here the old distinction "exoteric-esoteric" comes into play. This has become completely foreign to modern thinking. Who, nowadays, can understand what it means when Clement of Alexandria says[6] that the fundamental teaching about things has been kept secret from barbarians as well as from Greeks? Why was this? In any case, it is worth noting that Goethe seriously considered this

2. Seventh letter 344 c.
3. Ibid. 341 d.
4. 1341 a.
5. Summa theologica I, II, 2, 2 ad I.
6. Stromateis 5, 21.

inability to distinguish between the exoteric and the esoteric "a great misfortune," whereas he himself was able to accept and repeat approvingly the indeed odd statement (by someone else): "The truth should have remained with us academics![7]

But let us first of all hear the opposing voices: the exclusivity of the academic, in any case today a utopian anachronism, shares responsibility for exacerbating social contrasts and should by no means be seen as founded on principle and thereby encouraged. While there has to be an élite, it is still dangerous to separate it and to promote an élite consciousness. Precisely the intellectual leaders must constantly remain in close contact with the everyday reality of "the many." The concept of the academic formulated here is undemocratic, un-Christian and hence to be rejected, etc.

What is to be said to these objections? If "democratic" is understood to exclude "aristocratic"; if "democratic" is to be interpreted in such a way that the term "plebeian" is positively related to it—then the concept of the academic is an undemocratic concept. It would imply differences of rank, such that human existence can be realised in a higher and lower way; that the many, the average person, the majority, "common sense" would not have a say—let alone be the final authority—in determining what ultimately is true, good, and meaningful for the human being.

With regard to the "exclusiveness of the academic," being fenced off from the many does not mean *social* "exclusiveness." Our concept of the academic has, firstly, nothing at all to do with defending privileged education

---

7.   Letter to Passow, 20 October 1811.

for certain social groups. It is possible to consider "separation from the many" as an essential mark of the academic and at the same time be of the opinion that all educational institutions should of course be accessible to all social groups! One does not in any way exclude the other. The "Thracian maid" does represent the many, but not a social grouping. She can belong to all groupings, and she *does*, too (just like those susceptible to the "common attraction" of music); whereas, as I have said, the best aspects of the academic attitude can also be realisable in every social stratum.

Furthermore—and secondly—while the academic attitude is characterised by being distinguished from that of the many, it is not, however, an attitude *towards* the many. Undoubtedly there is a danger here which must be faced square on and combated by highlighting the necessary duty. But this danger cannot be avoided from the outset because it is intrinsic to the situation. Every élite is intrinsically in danger of being arrogant (probably all the more so, the less justified its claims to leadership); but the élite is not essentially arrogant. The unease the Christian feels when hearing talk about any distinction from "the many," and the suspicion that the pretentious contempt of small and ordinary people is not sufficiently under control (to put it mildly)—these concerns, which have unquestionable validity, are not relevant to present issue. First, "the crowd" does not mean the same as "the ordinary people." But also a person belonging to the crowd is, as a person, by no means excluded. The model of the academic only says—and this very emphatically—that a person belonging to the crowd can *not* be "helped" by having his way of life and his world accepted, but by seeing him as a spiritual being and helping him to appreciate the deeply unsatisfactory nature of average existence. This is precisely *the* educative task of the academic for the people.

Finally, there we have confronted the objection that it is necessary to maintain contact with the everyday reality of the many. The objection is naturally valid to the extent that it refers to "real" reality; naturally the "educated" person who thinks he can and ought to ignore the world in which ordinary people work and live as something inferior is a caricature of the academic. But we are speaking here of that illusory reality—although this is taken by "the many" to *be* reality. We have in mind the inferior reality represented by the empty attractions which serve the futile appeasement of public boredom and enjoy the applause and participation of the many. This all arises from not having the capacity for reflection, quietness, contemplation and leisure, and is becoming ever more promoted and widespread. It does not need much effort to understand what that means in the concrete (in fact, one would have to shut one's eyes and ears so as *not* to be aware of it): we are referring to the sensations of sport—*circenses*—and the latest products of the entertainment industry: the epidemic forms of killing time. It is part of the reality of this age that acceptance of this world of illusion has long since washed over all the social divisions between groups and classes that still exist. Naturally, academic thinking will have to look closely at this situation. *But:* opposing the credibility of this illusory reality and saying a clear "no" to it – this is exactly what separates the academic realm from the sphere of the many, and this for no other reason than in this way to make us free to see genuine reality.

If that which excites the many scarcely crosses the threshold of the truly academic and is considered hardly worth attention, the reason for this is not the desire to be different but rather to let true reality remain visible for what it is, or to let it become visible. Another reason is that for the person with the attitude of philosophical *theoria* reality looks different, *more interesting* than it can for the person whose vision is limited to focus on the everyday world. Making this distinction—which is "objective" and without arrogance and perhaps even humble since based on the awareness of receiving a gift—such a distinction from what "everyone" does and values should be seen in the academic sphere as something essential and indispensable, and therefore should not only not be viewed with suspicion but should be encouraged.

Naturally, after these sketched remarks, the question about the link between "academic" and "esoteric"—which has much broader significance—remains open. Here it has only been posed. It would seem that we still have to win back too much of the original substance of the academic before we can successfully form conclusions. But at least the task of airing the question seemed to me to be imperative.

Genuine objections draw attention to fundamental principles or conclusions which had not been mentioned and perhaps were not even thought about. They force us to say yes or no to such things. They enforce much greater precision in formulation: "Iron is sharpened with iron", as Thomas Aquinas loves to quote the Old Testament (Proverbs 27, 17).[1]

The following three objections are of this beneficial kind. They sum up the most important issues which, after the publication of this essay, were expressed in surprisingly numerous criticisms and gave the writer food for thought.[2] *It is not as if there was no area of outright agreement, but here we are concerned with the objections.*

That does not, of course, involve a claim that the reason for the question—which is found in the thing itself—can be dealt with once and for all by an exhaustive answer.

1. De perfectione vitae spiritualis. Conclusion.
2. For what I see as the most significant critical objections I am grateful to Joseph Pascher (Munich), Stephan Strasser (Nymwegen), E. Ungerer (Karlsruhe), Wilhelm Weischedel (Tübingen), Erich Weniger (Göttingen). Naturally, however, the author takes responsibility here for the formulation of these objections, even where individual phrases are based directly on the original wording of the criticisms.

Purity of the *theoria*

The first objection concerns the relationship between *theoria* and praxis which are too starkly divorced from one another.

Man is an active being with the obvious right, and even duty, to use nature and its forces. And so human knowledge cannot be isolated from the active realisation of goals, or isolated from praxis.

Yes, man is an active being. But what distinguishes human activity from that of animals? That the activity of animals is based on a blind drive, and that of human beings on decision. And what is special about decision, if not that knowledge of reality is converted into the decision to act? Goethe's famous saying means exactly this: "In action and doing everything depends on the objects being grasped purely and being treated according to their nature."[3] To grasp the objects purely: that can only mean that the vision is free—not distracted or clouded by any "unobjective interest"—and its measure is taken exclusively from reality itself. It is completely "theoretisch." Only through such a pure and receptive grasp—according to the ancients—does the possibility of "praxis" come about: human activity is human by the fact that it is preceded by orientation to reality and aimed at achieving awareness of being and "nothing besides."

Anyone, therefore, who defends the purity of *theoria* and its independence of praxis is thereby defending also

3.   Maximen und Reflexionen, no. 530.

the fruitfulness of *theoria* and therefore its connection with praxis.

But: in reality there is no such thing as "pure knowledge." The supposedly "purely theoretical" turning to reality follows the knower's prior interest. Perhaps one must say that such interest of the will in a particular object, such a predilection and loving partiality are precisely what make the right grasp of reality possible.

No doubt that is correct, but it is also not disputed. Of course, two things have to be admitted. First, that the interest of the will that precedes *theoria* is not itself already "action" or "praxis"; nor does it necessarily aim to be such—whatever it is understood to be (an extremely difficult question which, fortunately, we do not need to address here). Second, what is it that this loving interest effects? That our gaze upon the world becomes more focused, more sensitive, more penetrating; that reality—as it really is—can be more deeply experienced; that, in a word, knowledge can be "purely theoretical" in a still higher way.

But is there not also a practical philosophy? If there is, then how can "theoretical" and "philosophical" be identically one?

Thomas Aquinas does say in his commentary on Aristotle's *Metaphysics* and in open agreement with it: "That branch of knowledge which is wisdom and is called philosophy is there for the sake of knowing, and so is theoretical and not practical."[4] On the other hand, wherever *theoria*

4. Thomas Aquinas, *Commentary on Aristotle's Metaphysics* I, 3; no. 53. In the same work (no. 290) it says: Sapientia sive philosophia prima non est practica, sed speculative.

is realised in its purity there is an element of the philosophical way of looking at things. However, the philosophical *theoria* is something distinct and special which is not simply the same as the scientific way of looking at things.

What does this special something consist in?

That philosophical *theoria* can be "pure" in an incomparably higher way than *theoria* in the sciences. It is of the nature of the sciences that they view reality under a particular "aspect." But that means that they approach it with a formulated question. A person posing a question in this way wants to know something definite. Experimental science, at the beginning of the "new era," saw itself as coercing nature, as if extorting an answer.[5] I do not say that even in this case a genuine perception of reality is not possible. But a philosophical view of the world is of a quite different kind.

But does not philosophy, in its own particular way, also "ask a question," and does it not have its own distinct "aspect"?

It is in fact not meaningful to say: just as the chemist looks at things under the aspect of their atomic and molecular structure, so the philosophiser, in exactly the same way, looks at things under the "aspect" of their being real. When a person considers things as something real, as a form of being, as *creatura*, he is not considering them "under a particular aspect." Philosophising has so much to do with pure awareness that, in this being aware, questioning falls silent. The best and most essential attribute of philosophical *theoria* is the speechless wonder that looks down into the abyss which is the light of being.

5.   Francis Bacon, De dignitate et augmentis scientiarum 2, 2.

But this *theoria*, in such an extreme sense hardly distinguishable from contemplation, is, according to the ancients, intrinsically linked to loving attention:[6] *ubi amor, ibi oculus.*[7] A "purely theoretical" attitude must not be confused with the "objectivity" of a disinterested recording of facts. On a lower level of act (of knowing) and object (of knowledge) some kind of grasp of reality may be achieved—perhaps. But philosophical *theoria*, pure awareness, which forgets all undue questioning—this altogether unclouded mode of learning the measure of things cannot be realised unless reality is experienced and affirmed as *per se* worthy of our admiration.

All life of the mind—and this is true of "praxis" as well—has its origin in the process of becoming aware of reality and is protected precisely by the philosophical element.

On the other hand, however closely the function of the will—whether as presupposition or fruit—may be seen as linked with *theoria*, the inner structure of the latter is never altered by such nearness. This structure consists in taking its measure from the objective reality of being—in other words, from its orientation "to truth and nothing else."

Theoria is fruitful for praxis only as long as it is not concerned to be such—like Orpheus, who, when he was emerging into light, lost everything when he turned around to look at his success.[8]

---

6. Vita contemplativa Sanctorum praesupponit amorem ipsius contemplati, ex quo procedit. Thomas Aquinas, Sentences Commentary 3, d. 35, 1, 2, 3, sol. 3. Contemplatio perspicua veritatis iucunda admiratio. Augustine, De spiritu et anima 32.
7. Thomas Aquinas, Sentences Commentary 3, d.35, 1, 2, 3, sol. 1.
8. This phrase has been taken almost *verbatim* from the profound book by Konrad Weiß, "Der christliche Epimetheus" (Berlin 1933; p. 108).

The Philosophiser and the Ancients

The second objection poses the question of what philosophising has to do with "tradition."

Does not philosophising mean starting from the beginning, ridding yourself of all prejudices and ideas that have been handed down; "once in your life to doubt everything deliberately?"[1] "with a view to taking it back as something acquired by concepts?"[2] At least that is the way thinkers like Descartes and Hegel understood the philosophical act. And Greek philosophy—is it not similarly based on the coming of age of reason over against mythical tradition? Plato's greatness also consists in this critical independence. He does refer to a figure like Parmenides as admirable[3] but there is no question of an inner link with the "the ancients." A philosophical stance and "reverence for the ancients" are not only completely different things but are almost diametrically opposed to one another. Furthermore: since the dignity of the "ancients" is not to be based solely on how early they were, who is to be reckoned among them and who is not? And since also "integral tradition" seems to contain truth transcending the limits of time, what truths belong here and what truths do not?

1. Descartes, Principles of Philosophy, § 1; see also his "Meditations" I, 8.
2. Hegel, Vorlesungen über die Geschichte der Philosophie. Sämtl. Werke. Jubiläums-Ausgabe. Edited by H. Glockner (Stuttgart 1927), vol. 18, p. 69.
3. Theaetetus 183 e; here Socrates says: "Parmenides seems to me— as Homer would say—both dignified and inspiring fear."

It is easy to see that these questions are far more fundamental than the previous ones.

The answer can begin with Plato, under whose patronage this discussion is now placed. And the first thing that has to be said is: the "ancients" feature very decisively among the leading figures of the Platonic dialogs. Of course, they do not appear, like Criton and Phaedrus, as live figures; and as for Parmenides: he is not counted as one of the "ancients" any more than Plato himself.

Here, indeed, we have to distinguish between a narrow and a broader circle. The narrow circle is comprised of the first recipients, the witnesses and mediators of the truth which has "come down from the gods";[4] whereas the broader circle is comprised of those whose thoughts and teachings have fed off the truths and wisdom coming down from primeval times. Plato sees those witnesses and mediators expressly as figures standing out above the sphere of empirical humanity. It was given to them to "live closer to the gods and to be better than we are"[5] and hence to know things known only to God and, of mankind, to one who is on friendly terms with God.[6]

In Plato's work, "the ancients," as he calls them himself, remain nameless. For the most part they remain even more deeply hidden behind the expression, which occurs innumerable times: "it has been said from time immemorial."[7]

4. Plato, Philebus 16 c.
5. Ibid.
6. Timaeus 53 d.
7. See Josef Pieper, Über den Begriff der Tradition (Cologne-Opladen 1958), pp. 20ff.

And what is it that has been said "from time immemorial"?

For example, that God has the beginning, the middle, and the end of all things in his hands;[8] that spirit holds sway over the whole of the world;[9] that after death something much better awaits the good than the evil;[10] that the soul is immortal.[11] The truth, therefore, which the ancients know[12] concerns the totality of the world and the whole of human existence.

This "knowledge of the ancients" is, for Plato, not only to be revered; it is incomparably true. At the end of the *Gorgias* dialog it says: it is not given to us, "through our investigations, to learn anything better and more true."[13] And the words with which, in the *Symposium*, Socrates finishes his report about the guidance given by Diotima—this mysterious "Woman from Mantinea" speaking with the "knowledge of the ancients"—are seemingly un-Socratic: "Thus spoke Diotima, but I believed her."[14] These words express Plato's own attitude towards "sacred tradition" (by which is meant not just any kind of merely factual information that has come down to us but the truth, from a divine source, about the totality of the world.)

Have we not, unwittingly, gained more here than a mere contribution to Plato interpretation? How could we justify calling an attitude "unphilosophical" for which the founding father of Western philosophising guarantees

8.   Laws 715 e.
9.   Philebus 30 d.
10. Phaedo 63 c.
11. Meno 81 b.
12. "They know the truth; if we found this, why would we need to worry about men's opinions?" Phaedrus 274 c.
13. Gorgias 527 a.
14. Symposium 212 b.

that precisely this attitude is the criterion of genuine searching for wisdom? Or will one seriously think that concepts such as wisdom and *philosophia* are now, on the basis of scientific progress, in need of correction?

But could it not perhaps—from a "psychological" point of view, so to speak—be necessary that anyone who wants to arrive at real philosophising should at least "once in his life" use his own critical reason to confront all that is handed down?

Whatever one thinks about this matter, it is hardly ever going to happen that anyone will win back "through researching"—through what, in Hegel's formulation, is produced through concepts—that which he has refused to believe. The mythical story which Plato has Aristophanes describe in the *Symposium*, according to which men have lost their original perfection, their salutary state, through having brought guilt on themselves in primeval times, and Eros is nothing but the desire to win back this earlier original state—this story can justifiably count as a central part of "tradition," as "wisdom of the ancients." It is clear at the same time that only in such philosophising—enkindled by knowledge of the ancients—does the Platonic concept of Eros acquire its depth and human relevance. When a critical mind, trusting in no authority apart from himself, like Callicles in *Gorgias*, says that this story is "nothing more than a story" ("but I hold it to be the truth," says Socrates[15])—how could such a skeptic, through his critical thinking, "through his researching," ever again possess the wisdom contained in that story? How else if not through a new act of "believing"—which,

15. Gorgias 523 a; here it says: "You will, I think, take this talk (about judgment after death) to be myth, but I take it to be a logos."

of course, would have to be preceded by a now critically gained insight into the credibility of tradition?

Who decides what belongs to the truth content of tradition and what does not? What authority could there be in the world that can decide who belongs to this body of "ancients", in both senses? What criteria should be used to determine whether, for example, Kant is one of their circle?

It is true: "When we speak of tradition we are directly challenged to speak at the same time of authority."[16] To whom could such authority be attributed? Again, it needs first of all to be said that Plato clearly refused to make a claim of this kind for himself. Anyone, therefore, who in philosophising invokes Plato will have to follow him in this. Philosophy *cannot* decide on what belongs to the content of "sacred tradition."

Furthermore, just as the "ancients" are defined by reference to the truth to which they are witness, so too is this truth, which is necessarily incorporated into human language, defined by the reality which is revealed and comprehensible in it. But this reality is, as such, unfathomable for every form of finite knowing and is beyond all our powers of formulation. That is why it has to seem impossible to know, let alone express, the totality of tradition as a unity. And indeed there can be no genuine authority that would ever make such a claim.[17] One can more readily know and say what does *not* belong to that original truth

16. Goethe's Farbenlehre. Insel edition (edited by Gunther Ipsen), p. 553.
17. For example, the encyclical "Humani generis" (12.8.1950) expressly states, "the font of teaching revealed by God" can "never really be completely exhausted" by the interpretations of the theologians (cap. 21).

content, just as it is easier to say who does not belong to that circle than to say who does. Those who categorically reject tradition; those who expressly deny the Aristophanes myth and claim that man was never damaged by any primeval fateful event could be identified as not belonging to the sphere of the *philosophia perennis*. Then there is Augustine's idea of those who, though "outside the walls," nevertheless belong; and there is his idea of the dangers of all kinds of ownership.

This does not dispute that there really does exist an authority which has the duty and the capacity to safeguard the purity of tradition?

No, this is not disputed. There is such an authority. And also to support this thesis we have recourse again to information found in Plato. It is so clear that it gives a satisfactory answer to the question raised here. More than once Plato has said in whom this authority is to be found. In whom, then? In those "who are wise in divine things."[18]

There is nothing to be added to Plato's statement.

So there are human beings who have such divine wisdom? Who would they be? How does one know them?

That the answer to these questions could have become obscured in the general consciousnesss of the West, for whatever reasons; that the answer could become shrouded in doubt, debatable, incomprehensible and therefore impossible—this fact indicates, of course, the most profound cause of the rootlessness of philosophy in the new era.

18. Meno 81 a.

A new rootedness in cult?
The third objection is less an argument than a question—
one which, by the way, can hardly be answered.

Must one not simply accept as fact that the link between philosophising and cult no longer exists? Could not the task consist in providing a new foundation of another, metaphysical kind for "thinking which is no longer underpinned by cult"?

Of course it is necessary to know the facts as they are, but the true situation is hardly adequately expressed in its full extent by saying that a link that existed earlier has since been undone. The situation is only to some extent seen for what it is when there is clarity not only about the fact that in the consistently totalitarian work mentality there can simply be no "sacred sphere," "no cultic sanctuary"—something which in human history up until now is quite unheard of. It must also, above all, be considered that not only has philosophy lost the link with cult and in consequence the most profound guarantee of freedom for *theoria*, but that a reversal of the original relationship has taken place. The absurdity has occurred that the philosophy of the new era has declared this loss of freedom as—freedom!

We must not deceive ourselves about this. Surely knowing and acknowledging are two different things.

But what could be done?

Anyone who becomes involved with this question is inevitably faced with fundamental and absolute opinions.

That means that the possibility of a genuine debate disappears. So I can say that, for me, it is simply not possible to discuss the opinion that cult as a liberating force can be replaced by something else. Cultic celebration is, as Plato has incomparably expressed it in his late work,[1] *the* "breathing space": there is no other. Man cannot find his ultimate stance within himself; the place where the optic nerve enters the eye is blind. In other words, the origin in which the creature, "returning home," can alone experience satisfaction, *quietatio*, is not in the self; this is simply the concept of creature.

But again, what can be done? Is there any prospect, anything to suggest that philosophy can put down new roots in the sphere of cult?

How does knowledge break through? There would have to be something of this kind. Knowledge does not come about through some act of the will—no matter how energetic. It happens when something "shows itself," "imposes itself," so that it "can no longer be overlooked."

Now it seems, indeed, that under strong pressure and heat of recent eras certain structures of reality have become visible which earlier were able to remain hidden. Is there not something significant, for example, in the fact that in a recent attempt to clear up the terrain at present occupied by nihilism there is talk of the space for sacrifice as of the only undamaged area in a ravaged landscape? This utterance[2] in which, however, the refuge is called a

1. Laws 2; 653 c.
2. Ernst Jünger, Über die Linie, 3rd edition (Frankfurt 1951), pp. 10, 27, 33. In the same writer's work which appeared shortly afterwards, "Der Waldgang" (Frankfurt 1951), on p. 90 it is mentioned as a fact "that young people are beginning to deal with cults in a new way." (The plural—"cults"—is not beyond suspicion.)

"wilderness" is only of interest to us insofar as, diagnostically, it describes an existing state of affairs—which has a certain exciting significance. And there is some justification here to speak of a "starting point."

Of course, it is not satisfactory to see the realm of cult as an enclave which, purely factually, is a point left intact in the surrounding external destruction. Instead, it is a question of understanding the inviolability of this space as something internal, and only in this way seeing the truth about it. What is above all important is to partake of this inviolability.

Also in this respect we can, I believe, speak of "beginnings." Thus, in this age it is again possible to see the meaning of "feast";[3] and to see that the genuine, true aspect of feast in the most precise meaning of the word is realised through and in the context of cult. Our gaze, pure and freed of illusion through extremely painful experiences, begins to see for the first time that room to breathe in freedom only comes through sacrifice and that whoever is included in the perfect sacrifice as such has thereby access to the free centre of creation as to an unending festival.

This incipient rediscovery is a process within theology (and research in the history of religion). But its connection with what one can call the inner situation of man in this era can hardly be denied. And that again means a chance and a "beginning."

Naturally, for this chance and this beginning to be realised, for the morning breeze of this new-old truth to penetrate also into the realm of philosophising, awakening in the philosophisers themselves the memory that

3. See Josef Pieper, Zustimmung zur Welt. Eine Theorie des Festes (Munich 1963).

they can only focus properly on their proper object, the totality of the world, when looking at it from the free and festive centre of creation—here nothing can "be done." One can only hope that it will come about.

OPENNESS FOR THE TOTALITY

OF THINGS

*   This is the text of a lecture held in January 1963 in the Bochum
    Kammerspiele, in the city in which the "Ruhr University" was
    being established.

Experiences behind the institutions

The great institutions are accustomed to be the expression of great experiences—experiences which, so to speak, permeate them and consequently to some extent remain hidden in them. This, precisely, is one of the reasons why it is so difficult to define exhaustively the importance of the institutions which condition public life and provide the umbrella under which it is played out. It is not possible to say by looking at external manifestations of institutions in the concrete here and now what they are and what they are really meant to be. To be able to say that, one would have to penetrate, in a cautious and patient effort at interpretation, down to those experiences, insights and convictions which have been incorporated into the institutions and on the basis of which they are justified and legitimised.

But with relation to the great human experiences which make up our lives – experiences regarding ourselves and also regarding the world—it is not possible, just when we feel like it, to grasp them easily and to formulate them. They are not at all available to our conscious reflection. We know much more than we are immediately able to express in precise words; and perhaps what we say, factually, does not rhyme with our real conviction. Precisely this is the problem with opinion polls when they refer to subjects concerning not external but internal existence. The answers reflect what people *consider* to be their opinion, whereas their true opinion withdraws and remains hidden from such hasty questioning. "Do you believe in immortality?" (This was the theme of an international survey carried out recently.) It does not mean very much that in Germany 47 per cent answered affirmatively. What a person really thinks about immortality will possibly only become clear to him (perhaps to his own surprise) in a moment of existential crisis. A fleeting interview has little prospect of penetrating through at all to the dimension where such convictions are situated. Precisely our most vital certainties regarding the root of our inner selves and of the world, certainties so stable that we lead our lives according to them—precisely the great existential experiences are such that they are transformed into living existence; they are, in normal circumstances, immediately "realised." For example, they permeate, as I have said, the structures in which the life of people is lived and shown in history. Without being directly known for what they are, they are present and at work. Whoever wants to formulate them has to try to go behind their foreground manifestation and, so to speak, translate them back into a statement.

There is much to suggest that precisely that institutional shape of an institute of "higher learning" which we call "university" is one of those realisations in which great human experiences, touching the depths, finds expression. And one can suppose that that which makes a university to be a university can similarly not be discovered by a mere factual description but by the attempt to have sight of the invisible existential experiences which have been absorbed into the institution of the university.

With this we have defined fairly accurately what we are aiming at in the following discussion. I would like to try to formulate something of the experiences, insights and convictions that have been incorporated in the universities of the West and on the basis of which this institution is founded and authenticated. Here I am above all concerned with those elements of that prior insight which in our current era are liable to be endangered, overlooked, or given a new interpretation. It is again and again necessary to do this—to see what the impulses are from which the institutions genuinely live and on which they will continue to depend. To ascertain this would be meaningful even if what has come down to us were seen to be valid and effective. But the situation is now such that we are not only faced with the task of remodeling but also of establishing new universities. We need, therefore, to carry over the core of what was originally intended into the remodeled and new universities and to realise it anew. Naturally the question arises: will such a need be identified and felt to be such? Does anyone want it at all?

In any case, the traditional name "university" is still to be given to the new foundations. There is no difference of opinion about that. But this name contains, as everyone knows, a word which is fundamental to human language: *universum.* And the meaning of such fundamental words cannot simply be changed at will. How can *universum* suddenly mean something new, something that no longer means the one unified totality of the real as such! And so it is clearly not up to us to take the concept of a university to mean something totally unrelated to that to which this fundamental word refers. And really, however much our universities today—as is to be expected—are, in their concrete manifestations, distinguished from the universities of medieval Christendom, they still realise the same basic conception expressed in the name *"universitas,"* which means that they are institutions concerned in a unique way with the totality of things—with the whole of the world.

When indeed the schools of Paris, Oxford, Padua, etc. started to call themselves "university" from the beginning of the thirteenth century they were in no way seeing themselves as something new but as the continuation and development of the school at the grove of Akádemos, which Plato, the ancestor of all Western philosophers, founded in Athens one and a half millennia previously.[1] In my opinion, history has paid too little attention to the fact that the founders of the Western education systems, since the great Alcuin, have time and again referred to Plato's Academy as a model for their own planning. Of course, the detail is not relevant here; but it is an important fact that Plato's foundation also saw itself as *universitas*, as a teaching and learning society of people "whose soul"—as the Socrates of Plato's *Politeia*[2] says—"is always poised to reach out for the totality, the divine and the human."

---

1. See E. Gilson, L'humanisme médieval.
2. 486 a 5.

Spirit as receptivity to the totality of the world

Here we need to speak at last of the fundamental experience which is embodied in this cultural institution of global European society—an institution which has endured for more than two thousand years. The institution sees itself as ultimately rooted in this experience which is nothing less than experience of the nature of the human spirit. It can be formulated as follows: of its essence, spirit has to do with the whole of reality. It *is* fundamentally nothing but the capacity for relating to the totality of what is real. It is capable of and oriented to coming in contact and remaining in contact with absolutely everything that is.[1] "To be spirit," "to be a spiritually gifted person" means above all: to be *capax universi*, able to take hold of and be receptive to the whole of the world; not, like the animals, locked into a limited sector of an "environment," but existing in the presence of total reality, *vis-à-vis de l'univers*. This thought has been expressed innumerable times, from antiquity down to the present. When Aristotle says that the soul is really "everything," *anima quodammodo omnia;*[2] when Thomas Aquinas attributes to the human spirit the natural power *convenire cum omni ente,*[3] "to come together," to enter a positive relationship with every being; and when, finally, Max Scheler

1. See Josef Pieper, Was heißt Philosophieren? 5th edition (Munich 1963), pp. 42 ff.
2. Aristotle, On the Soul 3, 8; 431 b.
3. Thomas Aquinas, Quaest. Disput. de veritate 1, 1.

speaks[4] of the spirit's "openness to the world" and of its "having world," they all mean the same thing. But, furthermore, this is meant as well: that a spiritual being—and so, a human being—realises his true possibilities in coming to see reality as a whole and expressly opening himself to it. The development of the genuinely and distinctively human—in other words, the real education of man—happens only insofar as such confrontation with the whole of being is expressly set in motion. A truly educated person is one who knows his relationship to the world as a whole, however imperfect such knowledge may be (about which there is still something to say.

Therefore, as long as it appears meaningful and necessary to a group of people that there be—along with quite indispensable institutions for professional training, ensuring competence, education and instruction serving to secure existence and to provide the necessities of life (in the broadest sense)—also a "high school" in the fullest sense which has the highest aspirations to develop all that is genuinely human—the necessity of an institution which expressly and methodically aims at confronting man with the totality of being will also be clear. And this institution is the university. What makes it a university is not – science! But? But the definite orientation of its thinking to the *universum*, to the unified totality of things; the absolute and persistent striving for openness to the totality—that striving, therefore, which has perennially been understood and characterised as philosophising.

---

4. Max Scheler, Die Stellung des Menschen im Kosmos (Darmstadt 1928), p. 47. See also Josef Pieper, Wahrheit der Dinge. Eine Untersuchung zur Anthropologie des Hochmittelalters, 3rd edition (Munich 1957), pp. 96ff.

With this thesis, which introduces an extremely complicated matter and is, unfortunately, not as triumphally unambiguous as it might at first seem to be, we find ourselves in the middle of a debate. But before we take part in it we need some clarification about what is precisely understood here by philosophy and philosophising—and what is understood by science.

Philosophising means directing one's gaze to the totality that confronts us, in an exact and methodically disciplined mental effort to discuss the question about its ultimate meaning. Alfred North Whitehead (died 1947), the eminent philosopher at Harvard University and founder of modern mathematical logic (for which reason he could not easily be suspected of lack of precision in expressing his views), said[5] in his final years that philosophy's question is nothing more than "what is it all about?," what is the totality all about? He sees this as a very simple question, but one which also cannot be answered once and for all. On the other hand, no science asks: what about the totality? The sciences ask: what is the cause of a particular sickness? How did a particular historical event come about? What is the nature of the structure of the atom?—and so on. Science is constituted as a particular discipline by the formulation of the specific aspect under which it is to examine reality. Each of the sciences exists, so to speak, precisely through its distinction from other sciences. When the physicist, as physicist, focuses on some piece of material he is expressly not interested in the aspects which are of interest to the chemist or the physiologist. The philosophiser, on the other hand,

---

5. Philosophical Review, no. 46 (1937), p. 178; also, the same, Adventures of Ideas, 15th edition (New York 1956), p. 203.

even when he is focusing on something in concrete reality (and, of course, he is not always speaking explicitly and exclusively of "the world as a whole"!), inquires (no matter whether it is a question of this piece of paper, or myself, or one of my audience, or a political event, or a religious act, or death): what is "this here" from every conceivable angle? (And here it is perhaps not clear exactly what angles are conceivable; even that has to remain open!) Whitehead expressed the same thing as follows: *the philosophical problem is "to conceive a complete fact";* one can also say: conceive it all around, through and through. I said just now that the philosophiser does not always ask explicitly about the totality of the world. Now I must immediately make a slight correction. In the same moment as I attempt to know a complete fact (or to know a fact completely), no matter how particular or specific it may be, I am already involved with the whole of reality and all its relationships. I am unable to avoid speaking of "everything under the sun." As long as I am asking from a physiological point of view what happens when a person dies—i.e., as long as I, as a scientist, formulate a part aspect—I am no longer required, nor even permitted, to talk about "everything under the sun"; I would clearly be doing something unscientific. But as soon as I ask: what is happening when a person dies, what is death, not just from a physiological point of view but from every conceivable angle—as soon as I ask philosophically, I am by the same token talking about the whole context of the world and of life; it would be unphilosophical not to do so.

If, by asking the truly philosophical question the human spirit opens itself, without any reservations, to the whole of being, then he, too, enters the realm of his own

possibilities: the *convenire cum omni ente* comes into operation, which constitutes the nature of spirit.

And precisely this conviction—and this, again, is our
thesis—has been expressed and embodied in the Western
university, with the result that this institution receives its
decisive character and shape not so much from science as
from the living realisation of a philosophising relationship
to the world. And also the claim to be a "high school" in
the sense we have outlined, a place of education *per se*,
where the development of the truly human takes place—
this claim is legitimised by the fact that the ultimate possibilities of the spirit can only be aroused in confrontation
with total reality.

The role of the sciences

This issue is, as we know, not exactly without controversy, and occasionally one will hear something like the following: of course teaching and research concerning the whole of reality is central to the task of the university. But this task, in fact, falls to the specialized and collaborative work of the individual disciplines. The aim of philosophy in the old sense of the word is indeed taken into account. On the other hand, it is clear that the "whole of being" cannot be given any final expression. The question of the ultimate meaning of the world and of existence has proved to be one which, in principle, cannot be answered—which is the reason that it is eliminated from scientific discussion. The various disciplines limit themselves, with critical self-restraint, to what can be known with exactitude, namely, the particular and the concrete. What they achieve are reliable, verifiable results and, above all, identifiable progress. It is, in fact, research into that which until now has been unknown. In addition, results achieved in this way are of such a kind that they can be made fruitful and useful in the practical sphere: development of new sources of energy, richer harvests, better methods of cure, faster communication, more effective military defense, and so on. From all of this its importance for human development is also evident: the pressure to be objective—critically objective; the exercise of control over all non-committal wild speculation; orientation to serving the good of the community.

Put in a nutshell, this thesis amounts to saying that the university is primarily a place for the sciences and their cooperation; their educational task is—to use Fichte's formulation[1]—to be "a school teaching the art of scientific use of the intellect." Exactly this is what makes it a university.

We are quite familiar with this way of speaking, and at first sight it seems quite plausible. It seems quite difficult, if not impossible, to say something conclusive in reply. However, this is exactly what I want to attempt.

I shall begin by agreeing. Of course the university is essentially a place of science; it cannot be considered anything else. It is also completely accurate to say that we owe our gratitude entirely to the sciences for progress in knowledge both of the cosmos and of historical human reality; that indeed the findings of scientific research are validated by an incomparable degree of certainty and accuracy; that, furthermore, these results are by their very nature geared to use for practical ends; they are important for life in the strictest sense; for millions of people basic physical existence is only made possible through science. Finally, no one will dispute that scientific activity, by pressing for clarity and discipline in its thinking, for objectivity, rationality, and integrity, can form people in a way that cannot be done otherwise.

But now the problematic aspect has to be identified. The spatial and organisational proximity of the individual disciplines is clearly not sufficient for the *universum*—the

---

1   See Deducirter Plan einer zu Berlin zu errichtenden höheren Lehranstalt (1807), published in the volume of essays edited by Eduard Spranger on the "Wesen der Universität" (Leipzig 1910), p. 8.

whole of reality to which the university, by its very name, is committed—to become visible to anyone. The university itself, as an institution, is not a someone who could "direct its gaze to something" or "focus on something." For that you need the individual person, the individual spirit. Only the personal members of the university are able to have the openness to the totality of which we have spoken. *They*, therefore, these individuals, no matter how much they limit themselves in their particular discipline to a defined aspect of reality—these individual students must expressly be enabled, indeed stimulated, encouraged, challenged, pressed again and again to turn their gaze on the totality of the world and of existence. For example, they should discuss the question about the meaning of human freedom—not only from the psychological, biological, juridical points of view, but as such, under every conceivable aspect; or, what literature is fundamentally and what it is for; or, what human death is over and beyond the physiological and the purely biographical, and so forth. There is no other way that the full context of existence can at all be experienced and become visible. A sanctuary needs to be prepared and kept open—expressly—by means of an institution which purposely and methodically plans for it. This is what makes a university a university. If it were not to achieve this it would be found wanting in its essential duty. It would be missing out on an opportunity which can be found nowhere else in the world.

Philosophy as the center of the university

It is clear that this becoming visible of total reality is not in the hands of science. It happens, as I have already said, through the way the philosophiser confronts the world. I need to make a few more remarks about this distinction—not only for the sake of clarification but also in defense (of philosophy).

First point: unanswerable questions are not posed by science, or, once they are seen as such, are eliminated. And rightly so. By contrast, the philosophiser does *not* stop thinking about and discussing questions of which it is generally agreed that they will never be answered once and for all. Fundamentally, what is knowledge; can we be certain about immortality; what does being real mean? We will never find an answer which fully puts an end to these questions, unlike the answer about the way the tubercle bacillus becomes the infectious agent of tuberculosis. But why not drop these questions? The answer is that the act of questioning is in itself a way of remaining in hot pursuit of reality and of keeping it in sight. It is also a way of openness to the totality—an openness which constitutes the nature of spirit. Anyone who refuses, on principle, to ask questions which cannot be exactly answered; anyone who refuses to do this, not only in the context of scientific investigations but as a human person, has already lost sight of the reality as a whole and has given up the possibility of realising his own possibilities in an undiminished way. This does come about. There is a specific form of narrowness of mind, not to say lack of freedom, that is entirely due to limiting the spirit to what can be scientifically known.[1]

Second point: the achievement of the sciences consists in their constant progress in shedding light on what is hitherto unknown. Every piece of scientific knowledge produces something new. It is a piece of "progress." The periodic table, blood circulation, the functioning of hormones—all of these are things of which nothing at all was known up to the point where they were discovered. But anyone pondering a philosophical question—the more he lets himself be engaged with it—experiences a progressive discovery regarding the matter in question (death, immortality, freedom, guilt and so forth); but that clearly does not mean that he discovers something which was previously completely unfamiliar to him. It is rather that something becomes clearer to him which he already knew, though far less clearly. This is the reason that Plato understood and described philosophical knowledge as the regaining of something forgotten, as memory. The question as to what sense there is in pondering the totality of existence if it does not really bring anything new to light can be answered by saying that it is necessary for us not only to broaden our knowledge of the world but also—and perhaps still more—to call to mind the unchangeable truths. Naturally this does not mean making a romantic escape from reality, but, instead, remaining wide awake to it, not forgetting or brushing aside any critically based knowledge we have either about ourselves or about the world.

1. See Joseph Pieper, Erkenntnis und Freiheit, in: Weistum, Dichtung, Sakrament (Munich 1954), pp.35f.

The third point is that by contrast with scientific knowledge the philosophical contemplation of reality has no practical aspect. It is not useful for assuring a safe existence or providing for everyday needs. It is not of such a kind that, as Descartes proclaimed,[2] we are enabled through it to become "lords and owners of nature" (*maîtres et possesseurs de la nature*). But the other side of the coin is more important: philosophising is, by its very nature, "free"; it is, of itself, a meaningful activity with no relevance to goals outside itself; it cannot be taken into service. The practical aspect of science also has its other side: inescapability and ambivalence. It is known that amongst the discoverers of atomic energy there were some who tried to prevent its technical exploitation. But this kind of science is, *of its very nature*, geared to practicality, oriented towards application and use—of both kinds: use and abuse. The point where abuse begins can only be determined on the basis of matters not encountered in atomic physics. And the provision of what really meets our needs in life presupposes clarity about what this "life" consists in—truly human life. Science is not adequate to this task. Here we need the philosophical consideration of life as a whole.

The fourth point concerns the power to develop and educate which is to be attributed to science on the one hand and philosophy on the other.

Science, it is rightly said, forces its adepts to think objectively, disinterestedly, rationally, and with discipline. No one will dispute that these are lofty and indispensable virtues of the spirit which are radiated far beyond the sphere of scientific activity. However, the performance of

2. Discours de la Méthode, cap. 6.

the truly philosophical act, if the circumstances are favourable, leaves an incomparably deeper impression on the person than "education through science" can ever do or is even intended to do. The philosophiser, if he wants to concern himself with his subject at all, is challenged in a much more radical way. Much more is demanded of him than objectivity of thought: namely, a gaze that is uninhibited and open right down into the foundation of his being; a completely silent attitude of listening; a *simplicitas* of the spirit which reaches down to the core of the person. In philosophising it is not merely a question of activating one's abilities and harnessing one's strengths. The spirit sees itself much more challenged to realise its utmost possibility of *being*; not just to do what it can, but to become what it is: receptivity for the totality of the world.

Openness to every conceivable aspect

Speaking of openness to the totality sounds very ambitious. But we are not dealing with a claim which one makes, but to which one exposes oneself and to which one submits. It is, with regard to the philosophical position, aimed more at modest self-appraisal than at any kind of "superior leadership stance." More concretely: the idea is precisely *not* that philosophy is in possession of the totality in a closed system of perfect knowledge. We know that this can in no way be taken for granted. I shall cite only the three great representatives of so-called "German idealism": Schelling,[1] who said philosophy was the "science of the eternal archetypes of things"; Hegel,[2] who understands it as "comprehension of the absolute"; Fichte,[3] who says that "philosophy anticipates the whole of experience." Nothing is so understandable as the fact that the empirical sciences, on the point of taking possession of their realms, would have to reject the leadership claims of philosophy as grotesquely exaggerated and unreasonable—that is, if they ever became aware of such claims. Such a presumptuous self-definition of philosophy has,

1. Lectures on the method of academic study. Published under the title "Studium Generale" by H. Glockner (Stuttgart 1954), p. 70.
2. In a draft of a letter to his pupil H. F. W. Hinrich in the summer 1819. Briefe von und an Hegel. Edited by Johannes Hoffmeister (Hamburg 1952), vol.2, p. 216.
3. Erste Einleitung in die Wissenschaftslehre. Edited by Fritz Medicus (Leipzig 1944), p. 31.

indeed, introduced tensions in the relationship of the sciences to philosophy even into current discussions about the shape to be given to universities. Such tensions are difficult to be rid of.

Confronted with this, one must go back to the original meaning of the word *philosophia* which in both antiquity and the medieval period was accepted as authentic. *Philosophia* means anything but the possession of that comprehensive knowledge that we call wisdom. Instead, it is the loving search for it—a search which, while it is never-ending is also not in vain. It is the same with the world and existence: in one respect they are clear to us, fundamentally knowable, and in another respect incomprehensible and unfathomable.[4] But because this is so the philosophiser is always going to be looking to every attainable piece of information about his object, knowing that light will never be shed on it once and for all. He remains dependent on the information continuously being revealed by the sciences. He is not permitted to say: since I am inquiring about the "metaphysical nature" of man I am not interested in what psychology, the physiology of the brain, behavioral research have to say about man. If he were to say this he would immediately have ceased any serious philosophising, no longer considering every conceivable aspect of reality. But this is what constitutes the rank and dignity of philosophy: the philosophising preoccupation with the totality of the world is what gives the university its basic shape—as we have been saying. But "claims to leadership"? What else could it mean? It

---

4. See Josef Pieper, Unaustrinkbares Licht. Das negative Element in der Weltansicht des Thomas von Aquin, 2ⁿᵈ edition (Munich 1936), pp. 24–41.

means that philosophy, while constantly needing to listen out for all discoveries of all the sciences, has to make sure—and it alone has this responsibility—that no single "conceivable aspect" is suppressed, neglected, hidden and not given its due place; in other words, that there is and remains openness to consideration of the totality of the object, of the "complete fact."

This commitment to an openness, to not being closed off from any achievable information about reality, no matter what its origin, has a further consequence. The question is unavoidable: does this obligation not also extend to information which does not stem from our own experience and research but from a sphere beyond the human—from sacred tradition, from revelation, from the word of God? There is no doubt that the great initiators and founders of Western philosophy, not only Plato but also Aristotle, expressly included in their thinking information from the suprahuman sphere. This is precisely what gives existential spice to the Platonic dialogues and Aristotle's metaphysics and manages to keep thinkers in suspense up to the present day. This firm unselfconsciousness in regard to theology is characteristic of ancient philosophy. It is based on the conviction that it would be simply unphilosophical to exclude on principle any sort of possible information about reality. For the same reason, a university without theology cannot be a university in the full sense insofar as one takes the term to mean a "high school" as such, which claims—and has the obligation—to present the totality of world and existence. The great nineteenth-century humanist, John Henry Newman,[5] has expressed this in a somewhat aggressive sentence:

5. The Idea of a University (London 1921), p. 42.

"University teaching without Theology is simply unphilo-sophical"; the exclusion of theology conflicts with the uni-versity as a *philosophical* establishment.

Here, too, it must naturally be added that theology can likewise misunderstand itself and its role within the uni-versity and that this is by no means a merely abstract pos-sibility. However much it is the function of theology to ensure that a whole dimension of reality does not fall into oblivion, Western theology still has, in its great represen-tatives, always understood that to carry out its particular task—the interpretation of sacred tradition—is dependent on all contributions of those striving for natural scientific knowledge. Even the invidious term referring to the "hand maiden" role in which the sciences were to serve theology—a term which has been misinterpreted a thou-sand times, and indeed by both sides—fundamentally means nothing else than that cooperation is indispensable.[6] Only a theology that does not avoid the inevitable conflicts and the uncomfortable confrontation with scientific research is at all able to understand its own theological task. If we keep in mind all the findings, for instance, of research into evolution, how could theology say to us with conviction what exactly is the true and un-alterable meaning of the biblical statement that God shaped man out of the clay of the earth and breathed the breath of life into him?

The importance of such lively confrontations between theology and individual branches of science taking place was drastically brought home to me recently during some months of teaching in Indian universities. In India, where

6. See Josef Pieper, Hinführung zu Thomas von Aquin, 2nd edition (Munich 1963), p. 212ff.

the whole land is vibrant with religious impulses, there is no theology in the universities. Not even the Hindu university in Benares, although it is built around a temple, had a chair for the theology of Hinduism. Such an absence, as I came to see very clearly, had many unforeseeable and dangerous consequences. The danger consists not only in the fact that theology itself and religious tradition quite naturally lose credibility and become sterile; what is worse is that the spiritual leadership of a whole people threatens to become alienated from the true origins of its own culture.

Of course, it is not enough to have the mere presence of philosophy and theology represented as "subjects," each with a faculty of its own, within the university. Being set up institutionally is an indispensable presupposition. But what is peculiar both to philosophy and theology is precisely that, by their very nature, they are not "subjects" like other disciplines. Both are, strictly speaking, not defined by being definite, clearly delimited "special areas." It could almost be said, on the contrary, that one who philosophises seriously is not at all interested in the "subject" philosophy, just as the theologian, when acting specifically as theologian, is not primarily concerned with "methodically clean" theology (although he has to see to this as well). The question of thematic delineation of one's own territory is for philosophy and theology virtually meaningless; both have to do with the whole of reality— and it alone. And this is exactly where their importance lies for the life of the university.

It has often been said, and no doubt rightly, that the "cooperation of the disciplines" is crucial for the university. But it is often overlooked that the individual disciplines are constituted precisely by each of them being focused on one part aspect, so that this cooperation cannot be realised by them. Such an expectation cannot, on principle, be met. That would require mediation which the sciences cannot supply. Only the philosophical/theological point of view is capable of supplying it. This approach alone, as long as the two are not treated as merely specific disciplines, can enable and continue the many-sided debate in which the true unity of the university becomes reality and is proven to be such.

Openness to "disputation"

At this point I would like to venture to present the only concrete organisational suggestion I can contribute to the discussion about renewal of the university. It is this: there should be room in the structure of the university itself for academic debate which spreads across the disciplines and faculties. In this I am, of course, not thinking of the exchange of opinions among specialists about specific questions which only concern experts in the subject. I am referring to the themes of the conversations about man "as man" (the binding force of tradition; right to artificial language; what is meant by truth; the point of theology; and so forth)—subjects, therefore, which, as is to be expected, individual disciplines are constantly finding questionable and in need of discussion. Precisely the readiness for such open-ended conflict I would see as a specially desirable fruit of philosophical and university training.

It is probably a romantic misunderstanding to think that the medieval university gave its students, as a matter of course, the "overall view." But there was the institution of a regular *disputatio* which, on principle, excluded no argument and no partner, and thereby automatically enforced a universality of aspects.[1] A man like Thomas Aquinas seems even to have considered the spirit of *disputatio* to be the spirit of the university. Naturally, I am not concerned with restoring in our universities the

1.   Ibid. pp. 109–126.

external forms of scholastic disputation (although one should not underestimate the worth of the formal requirements—that small rule, for example, according to which one can answer an objection only after one has repeated it in one's own words and has had assurance from its author that this is exactly how he meant it). But the thing that lies behind the external form, the regulated debate which, no matter how keen the contest, is still a conversation—this crucial element of the *disputatio* is a thousand times more important for the university in its present situation than it could have been for the medieval university. It is true that at that time there was no possibility of an harmonious comprehensive system for interpreting the world (it is not by chance that the largest *Summa* of the thirteenth century remained a fragment). But for us even the sketch of a Summa has become unthinkable. The diversity of our knowledge about the world has become so boundless that we are no longer in a position to present and justify a rounded and closed statement about the world. But this does not at all need to be seen as an expression of agnostic despair. Instead, this deliberate abstention can very well be aimed at "rescuing" the image of a world which, despite everything, is unified, and at keeping our minds open to the totality which defies all final formulation.

This openness to the totality is, as I have already said, not achieved by the simple fact that all of these specific disciplines exist under the same roof of the university. If it is to be achieved at all, this can only happen in the minds of the individuals who, listening and speaking, take part in the many-sided dialog between the disciplines. To be capable of this dialog and, indeed, to be open to it—this is exactly what constitutes the true university teacher. Over and above his scientific qualifications, he must be in a position to appreciate the relevance of his specific findings for the broader discussion which concerns the totality, and introduce them, without non-committal generalisations, into that philosophical conversation. Of course, this presupposes something else, namely that he does not refuse to bring his ultimate convictions into play where necessary. That which is not permissible in discussion within the disciplines and is rightly considered not only unscientific but even an affront to academic discretion, becomes unavoidable as soon as it is a question of expressly focusing on "the complete fact" from every conceivable point of view. This, of course, does not mean promoting or countenancing private confessions. Philosophising has its own particular kind of discretion. It does require of the teacher that he be resolutely uninhibited in meeting the demand expressed in the question about the overall context of the world.

Once that is formulated, it is immediately clear what difficulties and resistance one must expect to face in this sphere. Fedo Stepun, in his memoires, mentions an example which probably still has a certain symptomatic value.[2] He is speaking of a Wilhelm Windelband with whom it was virtually impossible to form a human relationship because he was "a typical German professor of his time," "i.e. a scholar and teacher of a scientific discipline," whereas Stepun himself was "a typical Russian boy who had come to Europe to solve the mysteries of the world and of life." Once there had been a lively discussion in Windelband's seminar about "Freedom and Guilt"; the result was a series of several possible answers which were

2.   Vergangenes und Unvergängliches. Erster Teil (Munich 1947), p. 122ff.

clearly not ultimate ones. Stepun then summoned up the courage to ask the professor about his own personal conviction. Windelband's reply was as follows: "that he naturally had an answer to my question, but that it belonged to the sphere of his own private metaphysics, his own personal faith, which could not be a subject of discussion in seminars. I felt," Stepun continues, "that I was surrounded by the barbed wire of hair-splitting methodologies and that it was impossible to break through to the sphere where truth was tormenting me."

This thoughtful story is typical insofar as it shows that we need not really worry about the possible readiness of students to consider the totality of things. The problem in this respect is not the students but the teachers! But we will have to insist on the fact that the issue here is what makes the university to be a university.

It would be unrealistic to conclude with anything other than such an open question—although this problem (namely, how to attract to the university important scholars who are, at the same time, willing and able to be true university teachers) is only one amongst many, even though perhaps the most pressing one and the least likely to be solved by any "measures."

Nothing has been said expressly about the empirical situation of our universities. As we know, criticism of them has in the meantime become part of daily conversation. My aim was something different: namely, to recall the yardstick without which meaningful criticism is not at all possible; and so I have spoken of the chance which was given to the university from its very beginning and which is still available today and in the future. Of course, by its very nature, chance can either be taken and used, or it can be missed and wasted.

Index